Laugh with 'Raf'

(Glesga' kids at sea)

Author T. Glen ©

Kames Publishing
Kames by Lochgilphead
Argyll PA31 8RZ

Tel. 01546 886315

Laugh with 'Raf'

Glesga' kids at sea)

First published by Kames Publishing 2003

Copyright © Thomas Glen 2003

Printed by Compass Quick Print.Greenock.

To my wife Vi, without whose help,
and support, the Glesga' kids and I, could
never have ventured.

Chapter 1.

Development

In the early seventies, authorities were asking if any individuals who had a sport or hobby could give some of their time by joining voluntary groups to help young people. The idea to help, took fruition from a chance encounter with a Glasgow teacher. He encouraged his pupils with simple navigation classes at school and asked if I could help by inviting two of his pupils to sail with me, aboard a twenty-five feet sailing boat that I owned at the time. The young people turned up each Sunday morning and were taught sailing and seamanship. They travelled each week from Kinning Park in Glasgow to Rhu pier near Helensburgh. They soon learned as they thoroughly enjoyed the outdoors, and a year later a voice hailed me from a sailing boat, it was my former pupil teaching a boatload of youth! With such an insight into the success of teaching youngsters from the City I was encouraged to go further.

Born in Bridgeton in the East end of Glasgow I had every opportunity to understand the young people of Glasgow and their ways. I liked the outdoors, which possibly arose from the beginning of the war in 1939 when as an evacuee I was enjoying the countryside at Skipness on the beautiful Mull of Kintyre. A number of years later I purchased a small boat and sailed on Loch Lomond and as a city person I was again, fully appreciating the beauty of the countryside. Having sailed on the Clyde for a number of years I taught sailing to some young people in the club of which I was a member. This led to my thinking that maybe something could be done, whereby youngsters from the poorer areas of towns and elsewhere in Scotland could also benefit from their time on the Clyde, aboard a large sailing vessel. 'The cause' was born and the idea gradually developed to where funding had to be found to literally float the idea and make it a reality. With four children of our own and my wife and I, plus spaniel, we had *all* to be part of the plan to work with the youngsters on the Firth of Clyde.

The funding opportunity arose when speaking of the proposed project to a Glasgow businessman who was sympathetic to the idea. He then told me to go ahead and look around for a suitable vessel. Scanning various magazines I saw a boat for sale in Copenhagen, which grabbed my imagination – a Viking longboat with a large vertical red-stripped square sail and oars, which had been made for the making of a film and no longer needed. Ideally made for restoring a vision of the ancient history of the west coast of Scotland and now pictured by us as filled with teenagers with a sense of adventure. This surely could make a challenge for those who often said life was boring! My wife however did have a few doubts as to where she might fit in and jokingly spoke of beating the drum to keep the rowers rhythm going. An American however, with more money than our budget allowed, bought her and once again we searched.

An advertisement of a large sailing schooner caught my eye

and some telephone enquiries were made. The vessel was berthed in a marina in Holland and arrangements were made to fly out with a friend who was a boat builder. Leaving Schiphol airport behind we went by train to Willemstad where the boat lay and viewed her at her berth. Peter my friend checked her over and gave the thumbs up. Soon we met three very kind Dutch professional people, when on their hearing of the proposed use of the schooner for Scottish youngsters they gave their time and energy to help us with the purchase and preparation of 'Raf' in readiness to sail her to Scotland. Finally the day came when, with some friends from Scotland, we flew to Schiphol once again. With Jim, a sea captain, Stan, an airline pilot and Alistair, a computer programmer I felt that we were well prepared for the different duty watches in the North Sea! Our sea captain friend had the nickname 'China Jim'. This conjured up in my mind, sailing mainly in the China Seas, but on enquiring of him of his experiences there, he laughed and told me he had been given the nickname, as he owned a 'Chinese carry out' in Glasgow!

Setting off from Willemstad we motored through the canals to reach the great sea locks that lay between North Sea and us. We berthed alongside a German yacht sailed by a German professor and his two sons and were invited on board in the evening; both the eldest son and his father spoke English. The father at one point spoke to his youngest son of some ten years in the form of a small rebuke mentioning how he was not able to join in the conversation because of his lack of English. The youngster's face fell somewhat and I thought that it would cheer him up a bit if

I conversed with him in the international language of humour and some tricks. Asking him for his German sailor's hat which he was wearing with the two ribbons hanging down at the back, I soon had him laughing as I put on his sailor's hat the wrong way round, much to his amusement. I then went on to show him match stick puzzles and soon he felt part of the group sitting around the saloon table.

His father had been watching the fun that his youngest son and I were having with different tricks and decided to join in with a puzzle of using coins. He then announced that he would give a bottle of whisky if we could do it after his showing it once to us. Two bottles of beer if we completed it on a second try and if not on a third attempt, we had to give him a bottle of whisky. We all watched closely as the professor shifted the coins in a sequence of moves and he hesitated at one point. I watched and noticed my friend Stan the airline pilot, note the small hesitant move that was crucial in the completion of the puzzle. The professor turned to me, - "there we are now, you do it" and laughed. " Oh, give it to Stan, our junior, that will amuse him" and I dismissed it jokingly. Stan then started very carefully to move the coins about and soon came to the crucial move and went on to complete the game. The professor was flabbergasted, " I have students at the university, none of whom can resolve this puzzle" and opening a cupboard he produced the bottle of whisky as promised, still amazed at the brilliance of these Scots! I wondered if a bottle of lemonade would have had the same serious response from a Scotsman – I don't think so. Leaving Holland we sailed the North Sea eventually arriving in Aberdeen harbour where some of my friends had to return home and an extra two crew were found to replace them. We had met a couple of lads who were building their own large schooner. They were keen to have some experience of another schooner and stopped building their boat to give themselves a break. Heading out again after taking on supplies we sailed North to enter the Moray Firth where we were welcomed by porpoises playing on our bow wave like a great Scottish escort home. Entering the Caledonian Canal we tied up alongside a distillery - where else?

My wife and children had travelled by train to Inverness to join us to complete the journey through the canal, down the West Coast of Scotland and through the Crinan Canal to then enter the home waters of the wonderful Firth of Clyde. It was a Saturday when we were leaving Innellan behind and approaching Dunoon. Then what sounded like a canon firing was the nearby quarry using dynamite but to us it was another 'welcome' and we all laughed at our interpretation of the incident.

Reality had now set in; with a large schooner anchored in Rosneath bay, not far from Helensburgh pier. Now all we had to do was to find the youngsters who said they were bored and had nothing to do! Going back to the Glasgow Council I presented the credentials of the newly formed Adventure Sailing Trust and spoke of the idea unfolding - were they interested? Yes, they were, and a small grant was received to cover food and basic running costs. Our family then suddenly grew as my wife and I took on an extra fifty-six young people for sailing on the Clyde. Eight groups of seven would join us for three days each month so that a return programme encouraged those who wished to continue. The whole idea was about to be tested and tested to the full, to see if it all would work from the youngsters point of view who were aged between twelve and sixteen years of age. Our young crews came from the large Glasgow housing schemes to start with.

When the new, larger Region took over, they decided to run their own outdoor and resource centres and our services offered as a voluntary enterprise, we were told, was no longer needed by them. Our businessman then decided to ask for the return of his funding that purchased the boat and running costs, allowing us a time for repayment. We knew a high level success of the venture had been achieved through finding the ideal medium in which to work with some of the young people from poorer areas. 'Raf' gave them a real challenge; there was no way therefore that the work could be stopped because of a setback of this kind. The schooner 'Raf' had been adopted by the young people and affectionately known as 'their' boat. The work continued with a loan raised for the vessel through the kindness of the Glasgow District Council and the remaining funding to the businessman was repaid. The Trust now owned the boat and continued the adventure programmes as before. The cost of running and maintaining the Trust's schooner could have been heavy if it were not for the large voluntary effort of carrying out the required yearly maintenance work since 1974. Again the cost of a Skipper, Mate and Cook's wages would have sunk the small funding of the Trust kindly given by some grant making

Trusts, so all the work was carried out voluntary with expenses met. My wife, acting as cook, made over two hundred meals and snacks each week in the small galley of some four feet square, working area. This voluntary method of working allowed many poorer young people to continue adventure sailing, as only their own personal expenses had to found.

To-day funding is required to meet the cost of a new replacement vessel. Large capital funding for the continuation of this type of adventure programme is needed, and although sought from many sources, is still found to be elusive.

The Region decided after a few years, to give another small grant. We realised that for a stable working programme over a good number of years the Trust had to become independent, as the youngster's programmes would be badly affected by this piecemeal support. The teenage crews were continually asking to come back the following year and we said that we would be there.

Chapter 2.

The Maryhill Mob went to sea on a ship they called the 'Raf'...

Settling down to sleep on board a boat anchored in the Clyde with seven high-spirited young people aged between twelve and sixteen years of age, my wife and I, had volunteered for something of our own making. During the first day one of our young crew asked "Is yer keel made o' lead, skipper". I was sure the new crew were ready to value it for us. "Iron" was the quick reply "and we need it to keep the boat upright"! "Whit aboot these shiny metal things?" Pointing to the boats heavy rigging screws. "They're made of gunmetal and hold up the masts, and should not be removed" was the answer given, with a wry grin. Any items of brass were also greatly admired. I was beginning to think that I might have to check the keel and other metalwork as part of our inventory. Finding the cupboard in the boat, where my wife kept a week's supply of chocolate biscuits, was however, even more interesting.

Laughter was the result of an incident one-day when a new group of crew members had a cup of tea and a chocolate biscuit on joining 'Raf'. They had each been given a chocolate biscuit with brightly coloured wrappers. "Ah don't want a green wrapper," said one with some others joining in. "We don't want a blue wrapper" said others. They were of course, divided by their support of different Glasgow football teams. My wife promptly unwrapped the biscuits and put them on the plate. "Right" she said, "now there all brown"! Their first lesson had been given.

Evening came and before getting into their bunks the young people decided to draw the small curtains of the boats saloon windows. "Why draw the curtains - we are anchored in a bay with only the hills around us?" I asked. "To keep any monsters from lookin' in", was their reply! Then as the night went on a plea had to be made -"Quiet lads! Lets get to sleep now, its after twelve midnight and you have been going on with your loud talking and laughing for some time now, so keep it down." It was futile; they had decided to keep the noise level going. Finally peace reigned at two o'clock in the morning. Okay, it was everyone's first night, but we planned a fast learning curve for our noisy crew for the new day ahead. The plan would enable us cope and establish some sense of order. Five o'clock that morning the call was made - "Everyone up, - let's get on deck"! " Whit's the time? Queried the crew. "Aw naw, its only five o'clock and we're still sleeping" came the reply. "Nae breakfast"? Came the hopeful delaying tactic. Soon all were on deck and their job was to raise and lower all five large sails with mast heights of some fifty feet. After two hours work on deck they were unaware that they were amusing the local caravan site as the puzzled residents spoke afterwards of waking up and seeing 'Raf's sails going up and down like Venetian blinds and for what reason so early in the morning?

That week, just by chance, a challenge was made by another sailing vessel anchored nearby in Rothesay bay. "Let's race from our anchorage and round a couple of buoys," said the other boats skipper. Our crew from Maryhill, with their early morning sail hoisting techniques perfected, laughed at the idea and smartly took up their positions. They pulled up the anchor as the five large sails shot skyward and now 'their' fifty-three feet 'Raf' was heading out to the first buoy while our challenger with three smaller sails struggled to get going. The Maryhill kids had won hands down and jokingly jeered as the second vessel arrived later with engine running to catch up with us. Congratulations were in order and given by our friendly competitor "I've never, ever, seen all sails go up at once, and at such speed" said the other skipper, (but then he never got his crew up that early in the morning for training!) Even when it came to rolling up the sails, there was some puzzlement by the young crew at first, until they compared it with rolling a Bar-L. (The name given to a small amount of loose tobacco rolled up very thinly in cigarette paper and named after Barlinnie prison.) The youngsters then proceeded to fold the sails down into themselves and rolled them just as tightly. 'Raf' must have been the only sailing vessel in Britain with the very smartly packed Bar-L look.

All the crews were trained in rolling up sails and tied with a heavy elastic bungee or rope. Small wooden toggles were at one end and a large eyes for the toggle to go through made each one secure in holding the large rolled sail. Should the crew not hold the elastic tightly they could unwind at speed and hit their faces. A teaching plan of visual impact was designed to impress the trainees. I discovered that my helper had a large false front tooth held in by a wire support, which he could dislodge easily by a movement of his tongue. The training was given to all the new crews as how to avoid being hit by the toggle at the end of the elastic. To emphasise this, I would point to my helper at the appropriate time and at that, he would disengage his front tooth and I would say, "That's what could happen, should you not listen to the safety instruction". Their faces were one of awe and wonder and we knew that another lesson had been impressed upon their minds! We never did have any accidents of this kind over the years. One incident did happen however, when a young crew member stood at the stern while the boat was sailing. Having been told never to stand in this position he learned more quickly when the large boom moved and pushed him overboard. Floating in the water with his lifejacket and the boat fast leaving him behind, some doubts arose as he called out - "Will ye come back and get me skipper"? The boats inflatable dinghy soon picked him up and returning on board and changing into dry clothes he then said "that's made me hungry - could ah have a chocolate biscuit"?

Not only were the crew learning but my wife and I were fast adopting a whole new way of learning from the young. One night the 'egg language' was spoken of among the crew as they taught another member on board how to adapt words with 'egg' placed within the centre of some of his words spoken. This was indeed strange; as this anti-authoritarian language was such that others and adults in particular who did not know of it thought they were talking gibberish with no meaning. The initiated could however converse quite easily with one another, so we listened quietly in our cabin as everyone had retired for the evening and my wife and I learned this egg language of the young people. This knowledge surfaced when two youngsters on climbing our pear tree at home to gather some fruit and were concerned at our spaniel that barked at them. My wife explained to them that the pears were not suitable for eating and that they should come down for their own safety. They then spoke to each other in the egg language but nearly fell out the tree when my wife spoke back to them in their own egg language.

Chapter 3.

Fund raising

Part of our fund raising publicity comprised of taking 'Raf' up the river to Glasgow. The arrangement was due the kind help of the Clyde Port Authority with a special mooring being laid for us. Taking down our large masts and re-erecting them by crane we could go under the road and rail bridges and moor her in the heart of Glasgow. We set about to outline her rigging with coloured bulbs powered by a small generator. It was then decided to make hundreds of paper pirate hats with the end rolls of black paper kindly donated by a paper mill. Our young volunteers set out from the Broomielaw to give the Glasgow children free pirate hats with the 'Adventure Sailing Trust' emblazoned on the front. The Christmas shoppers thronged the city and soon we learned of some of the Glasgow humour resulting. Children of one couple wanted the pirate hats and our volunteer was asked how much were they? Our helper said they were free and gave the children their hats. Their father learning of the free offer asked for one also. His wife looked at him sternly and said "If you think I'm walking doon Argyle Street wi' you wearing a pirate's hat – think again! Another helper spoke of a Rolls Royce stopping and the owner asking for one of the hats. Having been given one he then asked the price and when told it was free, at that, he was somewhat perplexed. " I must pay you" he replied, but was told that to sell on the street, a licence was needed. Saying thanks he drove off maybe thinking that money couldn't buy everything not even a pirate's hat!

The job of starting the generator each evening to light up at Christmas always brought questioning bystanders and one wee girl looking at the schooner all decorated with an outline of coloured lights on the river asked how many rooms did it have? I explained that on a boat, they were called cabins and the biggest was the saloon. Thinking for a minute she then said "Oh, so it has a pub as well! One day we were alongside at the Broomielaw where the steamers at one time set off to 'Go Doon the Watter'. A well-dressed lady with a fur coat, standing looking down from the bridge, saw my young son coming out of 'Raf'. She asked him, how did a person book to get on board for a cruise? "You have to be deprived, to get on board," he said. He thought that this was the simplest way to explain it to the lady, as he was still quite young. Alaistair told us later that she was somewhat puzzled at his reply and thought he was being 'cheeky'.

Chapter 4.

New surroundings.

The full beauty of the Firth of Clyde can only be seen from a boat and the peace and quietness of the numerous anchorages has to be experienced to be appreciated. There is the odd time however!

"Raf" was anchored in the magnificent Kyles of Bute. It was a fine evening and my wife had cooked the meal once again for all nine of us on board and the young people were down below while I worked on deck. Then a lovely large white yacht arrived and after pressing some smart buttons the sails were wound in then the anchor was automatically lowered by pressing more buttons and the owner settled in his cockpit and bade a "good evening", I replied likewise. I then wondered - would he think the same when he met our young crew who were enjoying their evening meal and would come on deck after washing the dishes? The answer soon came when the crew, keen to go ashore or fish, came tumbling up on deck. My new neighbour looked at "Raf" then pressed all buttons to start his engine, weigh anchor, hoist sails and disappear round the corner!

Still in the Kyles my wife and I decided to have a 'treasure' hunt for the crew and I went ashore with a small tin of chocolate biscuits and buried it. With treasure maps in their hands the crew rowed ashore eagerly to find the unknown treasure. From the boat it was hilarious to watch, as they were still all wearing their brightly coloured life jackets, and so keen to find their treasure. They were pacing out north, south, east and west as from the famous 'Ministry of Funny Walks' with the three smaller groups interpreting their maps. Each group decided to shout to each other and their voices could be heard quite clearly over the water. Eventually the cry went up "found it" as they shared the chocolate treasure and silence reigned for a short while.

An nearby anchored yacht crew laughed at the antics of our treasure hunters and fell about as I called them to try a spoof on the 'Sound of Music' song at the top of the nearby hill as they were all in high spirits. To my surprise they raced up the hill and joining in the fun I raised my imaginary baton to conduct them from the stern of our anchored vessel. The resulting effect surprised us all completely as they sang well together and hummed the words they did not know. An unforgettable day of magic as the sound of singing 'the hills are alive' from Glasgow city kids, travelled towards us over the water to us on board. The applause from the other anchored boat was spontaneous as the youngsters finished and we also joined in the hand clapping - Blackfarland bay, in the Kyles, would always have memories.

Chapter 5.

Changing ways

The simple humour joined in by all the crew and volunteers on board was very important and was considered as a good therapy as the enjoyment of many of the young was paramount to their well being. Some people to day could not believe of the Dickensian backgrounds of a few young people we met. Knowing how these same youngsters thoroughly enjoyed their new adventures at this time was most rewarding. Given the opportunity, the initial eight crews developed their skills and their character and a quiet confidence in ship handling came about. The spoke openly in the evening over supper and a trust built up for all those on board.

In the early days my wife and I would be asked if we could keep some money safely for them. We told them to leave it on the saloon table and soon they realised that they had to accept the fact that no thieving would be tolerated and their money would be safe on the table. This trust was soon to be tested as a social worker asked me to help her as her money had been stolen from the office where the group gathered. I asked the group when they arrived about the matter and withdrew to leave them awhile to ponder on the problem that had resulted in an extra task being given over to me. I would not believe that they had been involved and asked them again for an answer. I soon got it - "Dae ye think skipper, that we would steal twenty pounds and jeopardise oor sailing on board 'Raf'? I replied that their answer was okay with me and added, "lets get on with the sailing". The following month on enquiring about the incident a tradesman working in the office had taken the money, knowing well that the young people would get the blame.

Another week, young entrepreneurs surfaced, as we lay alongside Rothesay pier. A boat that took people out to fish tied up behind us and a box of freshly caught fish lay on board. Approaching the other skipper our young crew asked about the fish and he kindly gave them over. Arriving back on board I asked what were they going to do with so many fish. "We'll sell them" was the reply and set off along the pier towards the main road. Half an hour later the crew returned with sweets in their mouths and in their pockets. "How did you manage to sell so many fish so quickly?" I enquired "Well, we sold a few to some pensioners at the end of the pier but that was too slow so we decided to do a deal with the local 'Chinky' and sold him all the rest". Initially fishing lines were on board for the young crew to use, but these over a time, were lost overboard and sometimes even recovered when we hauled up the anchor! This all led to their fishing being restricted until one day at our home mooring a cry went up as a large spool of fishing line floated past our stationary boat. With one quick move of one of our crew, he dived into our dinghy alongside and lifted this large coil of fishing line. We could not believe our eyes at such a gift floating past our boat and the great spool of fishing line lasted for years!

One glorious day 'Raf' was sailing with a fair breeze and nearly everyone was up on deck enjoying the sun and the scenery as we headed towards Cloch lighthouse on the Firth. One wee lad appeared from below with a bundle of toilet paper and proceeded to throw it up in the air to get rid of it. Most of us were in the cockpit at the stern of the vessel and watched in amazement when the unknown bundle started to unravel as the wind caught it, and turned it back down towards us on board. "What is that?" I enquired and the lad said it was his 'bog' paper (toilet). There was one mighty rush forward by the crew to keep clear of the now downward and fast closing 'missile'. Fortunately it cleared the boat and everyone settled down laughing. I then asked why, and found out that he could not flush the toilet so he had rolled it up to keep the toilet clean. Hygiene is always part of the training with so many individuals on board and I had to commend him for keeping the toilet clean, as I could not really reprimand him. I then had to explain how when the wind was on one side of the boat he should have thrown to the other side where the wind would carry anything away from the boat.

Having sailed a little further it was time to 'tack' by changing direction so the call went up "standby to tack". To be on board and see the young people jump into action is great. They let go sheets (ropes), which allows the large sails to flap with a great cracking sound in the wind and all heads are kept down to, avoid the moving sails, as the large wooden booms swing across, and is a sight to behold. Soon the vessel settled to the new direction - then up popped our small crew friend with a second bundle of his rolled 'bog' paper and again threw it into the wind, as he was unaware that the wind was now on the opposite side! The rush of the crew was again replayed and fortunately once again, 'it' did not land on our heads!

With the toilet placed in the centre of the boat and next to the saloon where everyone had to eat, the layout had its problems and a procedure was adopted to avoid a clash of timing. Again, theory is great but practice often intervenes and it did one day when a young group from Bridgeton arrived. A television crew also arrived with Director, sound recorder, and cameraman with continuity lady. My wife made them coffee with some home baked scones and set it out all nicely on the saloon table. I was on deck with the television crew and awaited my wife's call to come below. Unknown to us one of our young crew had used the toilet and the first I knew of it was when my wife's head appeared through the saloon deck hatch holding her nose and frantically signalling with a dishtowel to attract my attention. The T/V crew had their backs to her and could not see what was happening. I had to excuse myself and started to open up all our deck hatches to clear the problem and thought to myself that the young crew member needed some 'medical attention' at the time. Eventually everyone got his or her coffee and scones in the fresh air!

The anchor was lifted as the cameraman filmed and the final sails were hoisted by our new crew members. The filming continued as our young crew gravitated to the forward deck and some sat along the long wooden bowsprit. They all then started to sing without any prompting from anyone and I thought 'this is marvellous' as it sounded like a sea shanty and would add an extra dimension to the film. Then

I listened closely to what they were actually singing and realised our very young teenagers were singing a real bawdy song! The sound recorder was working away setting his levels and I thought that the television authorities could not possibly put it out to the unsuspecting public and voiced a query as to how they would handle the problem. Later that week 'Raf' was in the news and I sighed a sigh of relief when that part came, showing our young singers who fortunately were muted with the music of 'Sparticus' as used in the 'Onedin Line'.

The community on board 'Raf' meant that the character of the individual could soon be seen. One youngster, whom I noticed, kept himself somewhat apart from the rest of us on board and attracted my attention. I spoke to him on various subjects to find a response that would make him feel part of the small community. Then he saw me putting in a screw in the woodwork that had loosened over time. "Can I do that"? He asked, I saw the opportunity through this interest and suggested that he could check the rest of the boat for small repairs and with the responsibility handed over to him, he changed to being a real part of the young crew and a 'Chippie' (ships joiner) as well! This method of working with responsibility given, often establishes a young person's confidence with the rest of the crew, as everyone held a small job of some kind and established a good working relationship between the crew and ourselves. This responsibility grew as the young crews returned each month and soon I could leave them to 'helm' (steer) the boat for short periods while I was below. On one occasion I popped down below to talk to my wife, who was in the galley (kitchen). The call came down to me – "Hey skipper there's a man in a submarine wants to talk to you". I laughed and said to my wife; well that's a new leg-pull! I called back "pull the other one" and heard the response from the cockpit. "Naw, honest". Moving then to the cockpit I saw he was not joking and an officer on the conning tower of the nearby surfaced submarine, explained that they were taking part in manoeuvres. He asked if we could keep to the west of the loch as our engine which was running at the time, was affecting their detection of other ships taking part in exercises elsewhere in the area.

Shore excursions with various groups were nearly always amusing. One such trip ashore by us, found an elderly lady picking brambles and the young crew asked her what was she doing? She told them she was going to make jam and was immediately asked "How do you make jam Missus"? She very kindly and patiently related to them how to make jam and for my wife and I, watching seven youngsters getting a lesson on jam making was new to us as we had stayed in the background while they all quietly listened. The lady then finished and started to pick the brambles. "Can we help" they asked and set about filling her bucket with brambles. She laughed as we did, when her bucket was filled to the brim within a matter of minutes due to her seven helpers. "I've never had so many brambles and had such a quick pick before" she said laughing and thanked the young crew for their help.

Chapter 6.

Benefits at sea.

The 'balance' in human nature, we found, was greatly helped by the experience of living outdoors and the general well being of the young improved as the days went by. The youngsters also experienced the wildlife around them in the water and in the countryside. They fished and swam and had the enjoyment of catching mackerel and cod, and in clear shallower waters when the boat was at anchor, they could look down to the seabed for movement of fish, squid, starfish and many other small creatures when we anchored in shallower water. They were also amused at the seals sunbathing on the rocks. One day a very large seal was on an isolated rock just off shore and the young people wanted to have a closer look. I gave instruction to quietly row towards the seal but keep a distance so as not to disturb the seal's sunbathing. The result was a dinghy full of Glasgow kids sitting quietly watching a huge seal who in turn had an 'eye' on them. The seal was happy to continue resting up on the rock while admired by our young crew members. The curiosity of both kids and seal appeared to be alike. We referred to the lifestyle aboard as a ' Huckleberry Finn ' existence - a very necessary natural break from the city to keep that precious life 'balance'.

On the action side the young crew had the thrill of the boat as it lifted and surged through the sea with her tall masts and billowing sails driving eighteen tons of boat forward in a great gigantic dance across the water. One crew member shouted above the noise of the boat plunging forward into the heavy seas. His group all were from a drug rehabilitation centre. He hung onto the rigging as the bow's spray hit his face and called to everyone "You could never get a 'high' like this from drugs"!! - And the words came straight from the heart!

There is saying on board a sailing vessel "One hand for yourself and one hand for the boat. This meant that in larger seas one hand keeps hold. Plunging through heavy seas the young people liked being at the bow and one lad would often stand on the bowsprit. A sudden gust left him hanging from the sail rigging by his hands, just like a flag, then laughingly shouted back "Could you do that again, skipper" thinking that somehow, I had made the boat lean further than usual!

Being new to the variety of boats on the water gave rise to a statement by one young new crew member following an observation by him. He had spotted a fishing vessel that had fenders for coming alongside piers and made up of a complete ring of tyres slung from both sides of the boat. Looking at it earnestly and turning to me the youngster exclaimed, "Dae ye know Skipper, he'll never sell these tyres oot here." The introduction of young people to living on board a sea-going vessel gave rise to such interest in other boats and their owners. As time went on the youngsters learned of the less embarrassing ways of approaching boat owners without asking what their boat cost them. They were amused and a little proud as they themselves were being accepted by other sailors and were asked questions of 'Raf' when they went ashore and also asked of their own part in sailing the large schooner. There were a few adults who jokingly nicknamed the boat "Riff- Raf'

Years later my wife and I have telephone calls from our crews who have now grown up, married and with children of their own. "How is 'Raf'? They ask, and continue to tell us of their family and their work. A few have their own businesses and one young person who was keen to help my wife in the galley and asked questions on cooking, is now a hotel chef and doing well. Another young lad turned up at our door at home with brightly coloured hair and asked if we remembered him. "Yes, we did, come in Jim and tell us how you are doing". He had a part in the play 'West Side Story' hence the coloured hair! The same lad when he was younger phoned to say he had bought a boat and asked if I would like to see it. He then gave me his address as a high floor of a multi-storey flat. I knew the Glasgow song 'Ye canny fling pieces oot a twenty storey flat' but I never heard of having a boat on the nineteenth! With some amusement I arrived at the address and thought to myself, as I stood in the lift, that there was no way his boat could get into the lift. When I arrived at the nineteenth floor I had abandoned the idea that he would have brought it up the stairs.

Ringing the doorbell I was welcomed in and with bursting curiosity I was shown into the room where the eight-foot boat lay on the floor. I was surprised as the boat was for expeditions and was cleverly made up of cane framing, jointed together and then covered with a tough material with an inflatable gunwale (edging). When packed it could then be carried on your back, anywhere. I congratulated my crew member for his successful new purchase, which was sold to him by a garage-owner friend who had discovered his love of the sea. He had charged him the princely sum of twelve pounds rather than gift it to him and allowed him to pay it up when he could and then gave him the boat and an outboard motor for good measure!

There were days when spontaneity ruled and the young crew burst into song. On this occasion they surprised us and started with a Hymn that had the verse 'Will your anchor hold' just for the benefit of my wife and I and then went on to a rendering of - 'Bringing in the Sheaves' - or so we thought, until it dawned on us that they were singing, in complete innocence "Bringing in the thieves, bringing in the thieves, we will come rejoicing bringing in the thieves" My wife and I laughed when we realised what they were singing as we occasionally had to deal with the problem of thieving.

One such small group was involved when a wristwatch was stolen from a shop and would not admit to the theft. "Where is the watch?" I asked and I was told it had been dropped into the water and as I looked I could see it clearly. "Okay then lets have a volunteer swimmer to dive for it" knowing the outcome beforehand! Immediately the group moved away and left one boy standing. I knew from experience that the boy had been lead to thieve by another whom I had noticed was a ringleader and troublemaker. The lad could swim and dived in but could not recover the watch having tried several times. Our dinghy arrived to take us back aboard and I arranged with the shop-keeper to get payment to him the next morning. After attending to the payment I apologised for the upset caused and thanked him for his kindness in allowing the matter to be settled between us. I assured him that the matter would have repercussions. The culprits never did come back, possibly because they had to work harder on board after that, hoisting sails and pulling up the anchor and it's heavy chain by hand.

To assess the number of young people from Glasgow and elsewhere in Scotland who were troublemakers on board, not more than twenty could be counted of over two thousand who took part in the sailing programmes to-date.

Chapter7.

Further venturing

A group, one day, gave rise to Burns and his saying" The best-laid schemes o' mice an' men Gang aft agley". This happened when a group decided to get even nearer nature by camping ashore. After a meal in the evening they all, but one, went ashore with an adult youth leader who was part of the group. The one boy, who heard me say to their leader that there were midges ashore, (boats on the water are free of midges). He decided to stay with my wife and myself on board, with 'Raf' anchored in the picturesque Kyles of Bute. The tents went up ashore as we watched from the boat and off the group went for a walk until later. We decided to retire and closed up our hatches (openings) for the night. The next morning early we heard strident calls from the shore asking for the dinghy to collect them quickly. This we did and then we heard their story.

When they returned for the evening they had to get into their tents to try and escape from the midges. Once inside the conversation started. "What's that noise on the ootside o' the tent? "Ah think it's rain" – "No way", said the other that's thoosands o' midges batterin' outside tae get in! "Nae problem" says one "pass me the midgie repellent and al' clear them from the inside" "You've got the midgie repellent was the answer" "Ah, hiv'nae any – Ah, tho't you bro't it"! Said the other. With one movement, they told us, they both dived into their sleeping bags and pulled them over their heads!

Clyde Clubs come together for racing in the summer months and a whole mix of smaller and larger vessels compete. To give the young people a 'taster' of racing we entered 'Raf'. Soon we were in the cut and thrust as boats called out to one another according to the rules. An incident arose when a small racing yacht tacked near our bow. I was steering at the time and from the cockpit at the stern the same yacht appeared to be ahead of us. However our young crew often liked to sit up at the bow and after a few minutes one of the crew came back to tell me that the man in the smaller boat at the bowsprit said "He was laffin' " but he said, "he looks awfu angry"! I then realised that the word was 'luffing' and he had been luffing our bowsprit (wooden bow-pole extension) for the last few minutes. 'Luffing' is part of the racing rules and I had to call an apology for our delay in responding and turned as quickly as our larger vessel allowed.

There was a time when a large racing yacht tried to 'steal our wind' and I called on the crew to tighten up on the sheets (ropes). This they did and the other boat owner started shouting at us, but we were within the rules of the race and had every right to respond. Our young crew were annoyed at his shouting and quickly suggested throwing several things at him! I had to quickly explain that throwing 'missiles' did not come within the rules!

'Raf' was sailing downwind of an afternoon race of smaller boats one day; the last one attracted one of our small crew members. The boat was so far behind the remainder of the racing boats that he appeared to our lad, as possibly just being out for the day. A couple from the local yacht club were on board with the young man dressed with his smart naval white-topped cap. He was steering while his lady companion worked the jib (smaller sail). Before I could intervene, as my wife and I would sometimes do to avoid any embarrassment, the wee lad leaned across towards them slightly and spoke. " Were you oot fishun the day"? - No response came from the young man who was possibly saddened by his being last in the race. With no answer coming the lad looked at the girl and thought he would finish the one-sided conversation – Ach well, "Ah dae fancy yer burd"! A smile appeared on the girl's face as they sailed on.

Stories are numerous when young people show a side of their nature, which is sometimes surprising. One evening at anchor we noticed a large seagull sitting on an unattended commercial fishing boat with a large hook in its mouth. The next morning the seagull was still there attached to the fishing line and unable to move. One of our young crew members volunteered to go over and remove the hook from the seagull's mouth and explained how he would perform the operation. The two young people took the dinghy across and boarded the fishing boat. We watched as he gently lifted the seagull that was in a state of exhaustion. Opening the beak wider, he cut and loosened the hook from the bird's mouth. The seagull did not move as if it knew that it was being freed. The crew returned and all watched as the large bird continue to sit. Then it happened - the bird rose towards us, slowly circled above 'Raf', as if to convey thanks and then headed back to the nearby shore to sit for a while to rest before eventually heading off.

An occasion arose when in Helensburgh one of the young crew was explaining to me the types of pigeon that he flew at home and how the street pigeons differed through their poorer diet. With some deftness he put out his foot towards some pigeons on the pavement and gently caught one to show me the design of their wings and body. His gentleness I noticed, did not stress the bird as it sat quietly in his hands. After a minute he threw it up in the air to let it fly off. Suddenly a woman shouted at them as a reprimand for their catching a bird and I had to explain to her that the young lad was a pigeon fancier, he knew exactly what he was about and was doing no harm.

Working with young people has many rewards as the 'family' of fifty-six responded well to their outdoor 'classroom'. One young crew member that came from a stressful background had a test set by his teacher before joining us for a full six months on board. After this time he was given another test and the teacher found that he had progressed three years in his mental ability. We were asked if we had been tutoring him and we said no, but mentioned that he did appear relaxed when reading and was interested in the small library of books aboard 'Raf'.

One time I was asked by the crew, how long to sail to another anchorage? I saw the opportunity and gave them the chart, a set of dividers and parallel rule to work it out for themselves. The result was that they measured distance and time for nearly every anchorage we visited and did it correctly. This practical mathematics like their horse betting calculations was a way of life and not a chore. Some youngsters had not attended school for lengthy periods. I talked to them and explained about education and how if they wanted to get on in life, they had to go back to school. I made a point of it by stating they *had* to return to enable them continue sailing each month. This they did and I received reports with some amusing ones caused by their teachers' surprise at their sudden re-appearance and for their new keenness to learn! A few young people had been in front of children's panels and were often uncommunicative. I did get a report back however that bringing up 'Raf' in the conversation by any interviewer led to a real response by the young people who had benefited and a good dialogue followed.

At anchor the young people decide sometimes to play pirates on deck and started fencing their way around the deck. All was fine until one young lad not realising that the deck has curves stepped back and went overboard. Everyone wore lifejackets, so no problem, as the youngster surfaced, gasping for breath. "Throw him a line" I called "and pull him to the boarding ladder" Promptly another member of the crew threw him a whole coil of unattached rope over his head! He then looked like someone knitting a pattern of rope while floating around in the water. The pirate theme was played out on several occasions but one of the most entertaining arose when America's largest aircraft carrier was anchored in the Clyde estuary. Our young crew saw the huge vessel and it was considered by them, that maybe they could surprise the American navy as pirates. Soon they talked about how best to do this and retired below to hide and put on their pirate hats and gather their 'swords'. Their plan was to surprise a few Americans who were leaning on the ship's lower stern rail by ordering them into dropping their rope ladders. When 'Raf' came sailing slowly past the stern the American sailors saw only my wife and myself on board while they were admiring the schooner slowly approaching, below them. The 'pirates' soon came tumbling out of the hatches and called out to the American navy lads to hand over their ship! (The deck, in length, and high above us, looked like two football fields) The sailors joined in the fun laughing and said they would have to speak to the Captain first. The American navy lads would have a tale to tell that day, as how they negotiated with the local Scottish pirates at the stern of their ship.

An American nuclear submarine Captain returning to the Holy Loch was admiring 'Raf' and called out over his loudspeaker that he was quite willing to 'swap' his submarine for 'Raf'. We all laughed and declined the offer. We always welcomed this friendly banter with the Americans. One day however we sailed out of the Holy Loch and was intercepted by the figure of a British marine policeman aboard his high powered inflatable vessel. He had a call from the American mother ship based there, that our vessel had a crew on board suspiciously interested in their nuclear submarine in the large floating dry dock nearby! (It had all the hallmarks of an International incident!) He took one look at the young people with their binoculars, smiled and spoke to his shore base to say that he would tell them what had happened when he returned. (I guessed that he did not want to go on air for the complaining American officer to hear!)

Being on the water doesn't necessarily mean being in it, but it does happen from time to time. One morning it was decided to use a friend's large flat-bottomed fibreglass boat instead of our usual inflatable dinghy. On leaving shore and still in shallow water the crew complained of getting their feet getting wet and with one accord they all stood up – wrong! The boat capsized and everyone went in including my son Philip and myself. Another voluntary helper was offered the rope known as the painter at the bow unfortunately he was given the bitter end and promptly went down a second time as the rope played out. Everyone eventually ended up on board soaked to the skin and still wearing their lifejackets. Towels were passed around and soon we headed over to Helensburgh where my wife and I took the bags of wet clothes to the local laundry for washing and drying. I returned to 'Raf' and waited for my wife to signal me from shore when she needed the dinghy. That particular part of the sandy shore was very shallow and my wife, with two black plastic bags of dry clothes slung over her shoulders, decided to paddle out to meet the dinghy. A gentleman sitting nearby was amazed at this lady apparently walking out to sea with two bundles. I had seen the gentleman through my binoculars stand up, wondering what was happening. He sat down again when he saw the rubber dinghy pick up 'his lady of the sea'. Everyone then dressed on board and soon headed out for another adventure.

Chapter 8.

Making memories

One beautiful evening in Loch Goil, the vessel being an-chored and everyone having had a good meal on board, thoughts turned to a singsong on deck. Out came the guitar that was kept on board and the crew joined in a medley of popular songs. Then the question of an individual singer arose and one of the crew volunteered to sing 'Annie's Song'. The soloist started and his singing voice was good. The music carried over the evening air and another memory was made for everyone as his song continued to weave a magical hold on his audience. A farmhouse door on the shore had opened and an elderly couple stood and listened to our young singer.

The very next day we set off sailing up the loch with the wind coming from the bow and everyone noticed a bad smell. "Whit's that smell, something's honkin' " the crew asked and soon found out that it was our young singer's smelly socks some fifty feet away airing on the bow. "Bring them to the stern, where the wind is blowing away from us", I suggested, and this was done. Having reached our furthest point of sailing we returned with the wind be-hind us. Yes, once again the cry went up "move yer socks Alex and put them on the bow" as the crew burst into laughter because of a pair of socks had to be treated in this way.

Ghost stories were favourites in the evenings and we were

fortunate in having a helper Frank who, with an Irish way, kept the stories going at supper time. One evening he had taken the group of girls that were on board with their supervisor along the winding footpath to the village nearby. On his return with the group in the dark, he started to tell them of a local ghost that appeared, always preceded by the sound of a splash in the water and then a strange light. Our storyteller was the only one who had seen a figure with a small torch light coming, and just around the next bend in the footpath. With a stone he had lifted earlier and while walking behind the group, he threw the stone and the group of girls froze as they heard the ominous splash. The torch carrying man then appeared round the bend in the footpath and the girls' screams could be heard for miles all around! Next day the girls decided to throw Frank overboard while at anchor and as he lay on the deck they lifted his feet and arms over the guard rail. I saw that they could not succeed as his weight was on deck and quietly pointed to his strong leather belt around his middle. Two girls grabbed the belt and lifted him from the deck and over he went! From then on it was hilarious as he scrambled back up the boarding ladder and then on deck and all seven girls ran to seek refuge and packed in to the small toilet by locking the door. However the toilet porthole was *not* locked and buckets of sea water went through the window accompanied by screams from inside. Such healthy pranks gave rise to much laughter and everyone enjoyed their fun time at sea.

Just recently when 'Raf' was covered over with heavy tarpaulins for the winter one of our previous crew and his mate from the local village gave us a hand. His memories were of the time when as village youngsters they were cleaning the barnacles off 'Raf's bottom as she lay alongside the local jetty. Everyone scrapped at the hull as the tide dropped then anti-fouling paint was applied before the tide came back. Next day all our young helpers sailed and a great barbecue was held on shore. To this day such memories are retold and we are pleased that these years later they are still cherished by our crews in later life. One lad now married with children told us of his trip down memory lane as he had hoped to see 'Raf' again. He walked several miles as buses are not always available and sat down on the beach where he joined the boat each month. 'Raf' had sailed earlier that day with another group and although disappointed at not seeing her, he spoke of his sitting on the beach and remembering all the good times on board. Such is the strength of bond that can be forged with young people when they are allowed the opportunity to respond to a challenge of the sea with their peers.

A new group of girls who had been poorly informed turned up with their suitcases with all their finery. They had thought that a cruise ship had been waiting for them and I had to break the news that a sailing schooner awaited them and they had to sail her! Thereafter a rebellious attitude was adopted when they discovered they had to peel the potatoes just like any other crew. Sitting on the stern, two girls started to peel and a line of floating potatoes ensued as they threw some overboard. A good appetite is always the result of sea air and the girls that evening missed their potatoes on their plates and knew then that they were the victims of their own mutiny. The same girls on boarding wanted to know where the electric sockets for their hair dryers were placed. I had to explain that our electrical system was twelve volts and could not match the voltage of their hairdryers. They mumbled something but I assured them they would not have any problem, as the wind on deck would soon dry their hair!

One day, a new crew learned of their duties, where washing dishes like other chores are taken in turn. One young lad however refused and made a statement that he would walk home. I just knew that he could not walk on water as we were separated by the Clyde itself. To let him cool off and with a 'minder' with him, he went ashore. He walked to the end of the shoreline where he realised the water was separating him from the mainland. He then returned and had a late lunch with his minder, washed the dishes and got on with being part of the crew and enjoying himself. There was sometimes this attitude with some of the young lads that women were there for menial tasks and generally meant to serve their needs.

A new crew member having caught a fish told my wife he was going to use the galley to cook his catch. He was annoyed when he discovered that he was not allowed because of our safety regulations at sea. Having been refused he decided that he would take the steering manoeuvre as we came to pick up our home mooring. My wife normally steers when we pick up our mooring as I signal back to her from the bow without my looking back. The young lad told my wife that he would steer while she could go and make the

'Tea'. My wife told the story to me afterwards, how she gave the lad the steering to do, knowing the resulting situation. Standing at the bow looking at the mooring ahead I suddenly saw the mooring apparently move all over the place and called back to my wife as to what the steering problem was. The new crew member then realised that he would be wiser to quickly return the steering to my wife and in doing so learned that women could do things equally as well as men and his respect for women grew a little!

Chapter 9.

Our bravest crews.

A group of mentally handicapped youngsters came on board one day and their teacher explained that she would join us mid-week. The group settled down to a simple routine as we changed the working tempo to suit this particular group of young people. A pleasant cruise followed and confidence grew with the youngsters who normally lived a more sheltered existence. The outdoor stimulus resulting was such that when the teacher arrived she was amazed at the change in some of the young people. One youngster she knew, hardly ever spoke and now he was full of stories to relate to her. One young person concerned me somewhat by rocking while he was seated but this soon stopped as he started to enjoy the sailing and slept well on board. Confidence in themselves had grown dramatically for this particular group.

Another group of partially sighted children also took part and special safety lines were fitted to secure the young people while on deck. They thoroughly enjoyed the experience of the sailing with the wind in their faces and feeling the chart of the area with their fingers which had been pin pricked to enable the surrounding coastline and mountains to be traced, although they laughed when they discovered I had also pin pricked chart names as they were used to reading Braille. My wife and I were amazed as one lad, who was totally blind, having walked through the various cabins to find the layout below, could then walk like a sighted person with a confidence that impressed us, as the design of many boat steps and openings are complicated. This experience gained on board gave a quiet confidence to many of the young people and was an important part of their development. One sunny day as the Largs/Millport ferry passed one group of handicapped youngsters played on deck as pirates firing on the ferry with imaginary guns while the passengers waved back to them!

There was however, a day when no warning flags were flying from the usual naval vessel at the mouth of the loch to warn of 'loch closed for submarine manoeuvres' and this did, one day, create some excitement. Another young crew of mentally handicapped young people, benefiting from the Trust's sailing programmes, were on board. I let them sail the boat and supervised them as they stood at the helm and 'guided' the boat. As I have a skipper's normal habit of lookout, I spotted a periscope churning the water at speed well over to our port side in the middle of the loch. The submarine captain had also spotted us and immediately surfaced dramatically. The vessel appeared at speed with the great black nose rising first, then thousands of gallons of frothing sea water cascaded from the conning tower and around the massive hull as it moved almost fishlike with one great leap to the surface.

The young people clapped their hands and asked, "Could the man do that again"? The warning flagged vessel then arrived later to take up station, as we turned and headed south out of the loch. Glasgow kids, I thought, had done something the Russians could never do during the cold war – bring a British submarine to the surface.

Chapter 10.

All in a day's sail.

A day when there was no wind, the sea was like glass and then a shark's fin and tail appeared on the surface. These are the basking sharks feeding on the plankton of the Clyde. The young crew however spotted the large fin and tail coming towards them and thought of only one thing - 'Jaws' was in the Clyde. The cry went up "Jaws is coming" and some were not sure when I explained that they were plankton eaters and that they didn't eat boats or crew!

Anchored in Rothesay bay we saw a small boat with local youngsters fishing. The day was sunny and the water calm and I spotted a baby basking shark of some six feet approach their boat. (Adults can be thirty feet on average) Until then they had been lying relaxed with their rod and lines out and their feet hanging out over the boat. Then one of the young lads spotted the fin and tail! All fishing lines came in promptly as well as their feet, as they watched mesmerised when the young shark passed their boat and disappeared. They appeared to have held their breath as one great sigh of relief led them into a hysterical burst of laughter.

The idea of giving some day sails to the vendors of the 'Big Issue' was followed up by contacting the office in Glasgow. The outcome of this was that some of the vendors had a day out, from time to time, enjoying the Clyde on board 'Raf'. The idea proved popular and the home baking of large sausage rolls and scones made by my wife, even more so! One group had taken up photography and soon had several pictures taken of the boat and themselves that appeared later in their magazine.

There was some excitement one day when a fast inflatable powerboat appeared beside us and the officer in charge informed us that they were from Customs. Our volunteer, John, who was steering, jokingly spoke of being down to our last case of brandy! The officer then announced they were checking for drugs and on learning of our Trust's day out with the 'Big Issue' he seemed satisfied. The 'Big Issue' crew however learned that he had Custom's and Excise postcards of their boats and asked for some. As amateur photographers they possibly pinned them to their wall back home to show others as mementoes.

Later on, one of the female vendors looked longingly at the surrounding mountains and announced she would love to stay in a wee cottage in one of the remote hillsides. She was then told by one of the other vendors that her idea wasn't practical. "Why no' " she asked and the answer given was that she wouldn't manage to get her money, as postmen didn't climb half way up mountains to deliver 'giros! A year later I was in town and coming down the stairs of a Glasgow building. As I looked down towards the outside pavement I spotted one of my female 'Big Issue' crew and approached her as she stood selling her magazines. I drew closer and smiled at her saying " I don't think you remember me, - do you? She looked long and hard at my face wondering all the while, then burst out with the exclamation -

"Christl! The man wi' the boat"! I then replied jokingly.
Naw! "Just the man wi' the boat"!

The end

(maybe not ?)